CARL PHILIPP EMANUEL BACH

"Kenner und Liebhaber" Sechste Sammlung
Wq 61

Edited by Christopher Hogwood

Fantasia in F-sharp Minor
Wq 67

Edited by Peter Wollny

The Packard Humanities Institute

LOS ALTOS, CALIFORNIA

Carl Philipp Emanuel Bach: The Complete Works

CPEB:CW OFFPRINTS, NO. 63

This edition is based on series I, volumes 4.2 and 8.1 of *Carl Philipp Emanuel Bach: The Complete Works*, an editorial and publishing project of The Packard Humanities Institute, in cooperation with the Bach-Archiv Leipzig, the Sächsische Akademie der Wissenschaften zu Leipzig, and Harvard University. In addition to the present study score, the complete introduction to this edition is available online, along with performing material, at http://www.cpebach.org. A full score with critical commentary is also available from the publisher.

CONTENTS

Introduction · v

Clavier-Sonaten und freie Fantasien nebst einigen Rondos fürs Fortepiano
für Kenner und Liebhaber, Sechste Sammlung, Wq 61

Rondo I in E-flat Major, Wq 61/1   3

Sonata I in D Major, Wq 61/2   8
    Allegro di molto   8
    Allegretto 10
    Presto di molto 10

Fantasia I in B-flat Major, Wq 61/3 12

Rondo II in D Minor, Wq 61/4 17

Sonata II in E Minor, Wq 61/5 22
    Allegretto 22
    Andante 23
    Allegretto 24

Fantasia II in C Major, Wq 61/6 26

* * *

Fantasia in F-sharp Minor, Wq 67 31

INTRODUCTION

Carl Philipp Emanuel Bach's hint of a possible sixth collection became more of a reality by the summer of 1786, despite endless problems with the printing of *Die Auferstehung*, which by now he had transferred to Breitkopf, together with the subscription list he had assembled (although it appears that in the end the project made a loss for the publishing house). As a final hope appended to a letter, which also included lists summarising his printed works up to 1785, Bach added: "Perhaps, perhaps if I live and have strength I will finish my work with the 6th collection next year" (Vielleicht, vielleicht, wenn ich lebe u. Muth habe, beschließe ich mit der 6ten Sammlung, übers Jahr meine Arbeit). He was well aware that this was his swan song.

Two months later, on 30 September he was able to declare: "My friends really want me to come out with my 6th collection *für Kenner und Liebhaber*. It is finished and I have played it for them. It is not as thick as the previous ones, at most 8 sheets." (Meine Freunde wollen durchaus, daß ich mit meiner 6ten Samlung f. K. u. L. herausrücken soll. Sie ist fertig u. ich habe sie ihnen vorgespielt; sie ist nicht so stark, wie die vorigen; höchstens 8 Bogen.) Nor had he lost his enthusiasm for good commercial timing and shared postage: "If it would be possible for it [the sixth collection] to appear at the next Easter fair at the same time as the Ramler cantata [*Die Auferstehung*] how splendid this would be! The dispatch of both prints at the same time NB with the opportunity of the fair, just think." (Wäre es möglich, daß sie auf künftige Ostermeße mit der Raml. Cantate zugleich erscheinen könnte, wie herrlich wäre dieß! Die Abschickung beyder Stücke zugleich NB mit Meßgelegenheiten, denken Sie einmahl.) This time, Bach suggested, Breitkopf should keep someone else waiting. A

month later, on 26 October 1786, the fair copy was posted together with the familiar details of numbers, clefs and fine paper copies, and apologies that the pieces were written in different clefs.

Bach's own mortality also weighed heavily on him; writing to Johann Schröter with a list of his printed works currently available, he stated that the cantata, Wq 240, and litanies, Wq 204 remained to be published, which he hoped could bring "honour even after my death and much profit to lovers of the art"; after which ". . . I conclude my works for the public and lay my quill aside." (Diese Cantate, beÿ welcher ich vielen Schaden habe, und die Litaneÿen . . . sind unter allen meinen Sachen die am stärksten gearbeiteten Stücke, und von welchen ich, ohne ein eigenliebiger Geck zu seÿn, hoffen darf, daß sie mir auch nach meinem Ableben viele Ehre und Kunstliebhabern großen Nutzen bringen können. Hiermit beschließe ich meine Arbeiten fürs Publikum und lege die Feder nieder.)

In a letter of 3 May 1788, Bach wrote to Breitkopf:

I am not poor, thank God! I am not doing what I am doing out of necessity. I have earned a considerable amount with my sonatas. Their construction is not <u>that</u> which is <u>only</u> fashionable and soon forgotten. They are original, pleasing, not nearly as difficult as much of the stuff that is now appearing, and they are not old-fashioned. Enough, they will survive as long and <u>even longer</u> than my other things.

Ich bin nicht arm, Gottlob! Aus Noth thue ichs nicht, was ich thue. Ich habe ansehnlich mit meinen Sonaten gewonnen. Ihre Einrichtung ist nicht <u>das</u>, was Mode <u>blos</u> ist u. bald vergeht. Sie sind original, gefällig, lange nicht so schwer, wie vieles Zeug, was jetzt erscheint, u. sie sind nicht altväterisch; genug, sie werden sich, wie meine anderen Sachen, u. noch länger erhalten.

This is the last time in Bach's surviving correspondence that the "Kenner und Liebhaber" collections are mentioned. He died shortly before Christmas, on 14 December 1788, at the age of 74.

An announcement of the collection was printed in the *Hamburgischer Correspondent* (1786, no. 168), praising the constant novelty of Bach's ideas, idiom, and modulation (especially in the Rondos for avoiding arpeggios and enharmonic *Kunstwerke*). The dedicatee was Maria Theresia, archduchess of Leiningen-Westerburg, born 1746. The Fantasia in B flat, Wq 61/3 and the Rondo in D Minor, Wq 61/4 are the only works from the six "Kenner und Liebhaber" collections for which complete autographs survive.

* * *

The famous Fantasia in F-sharp Minor originated from an idea that was presumably notated already many years before. The existence of two different versions (Wq 67 and 80) seems to indicate that the work carried special significance for Bach. The original title "C. P. E. Bach's Empfindungen" in the autograph of the version for keyboard and violin (Wq 80) reveals autobiographical traits, and lends it the character of a musical bequest. The piece is based on a strict formal design that draws on rondo and sonata elements; therefore the work appears as a summation of the innovations developed in the collections "für Kenner und Liebhaber."

The music reprinted here was first published by The Packard Humanities Institute in 2009 in *Carl Philipp Emanuel Bach: The Complete Works*, I/4.2, edited by Christopher Hogwood. The Fantasia in F-sharp Minor, Wq 67, was published in 2006 in *Carl Philipp Emanuel Bach: The Complete Works*, I/8.1, edited by Peter Wollny. The complete introductions to these volumes are available online at www.cpebach.org.

Clavier-Sonaten und freie Fantasien nebst einigen Rondos
fürs Fortepiano für Kenner und Liebhaber
Sechste Sammlung

Wq 61

Rondo I in E-flat Major

Wq 61/1

Sonata I in D Major

Fantasia I in B-flat Major

Wq 61/3

Rondo II in D Minor

Wq 61/4

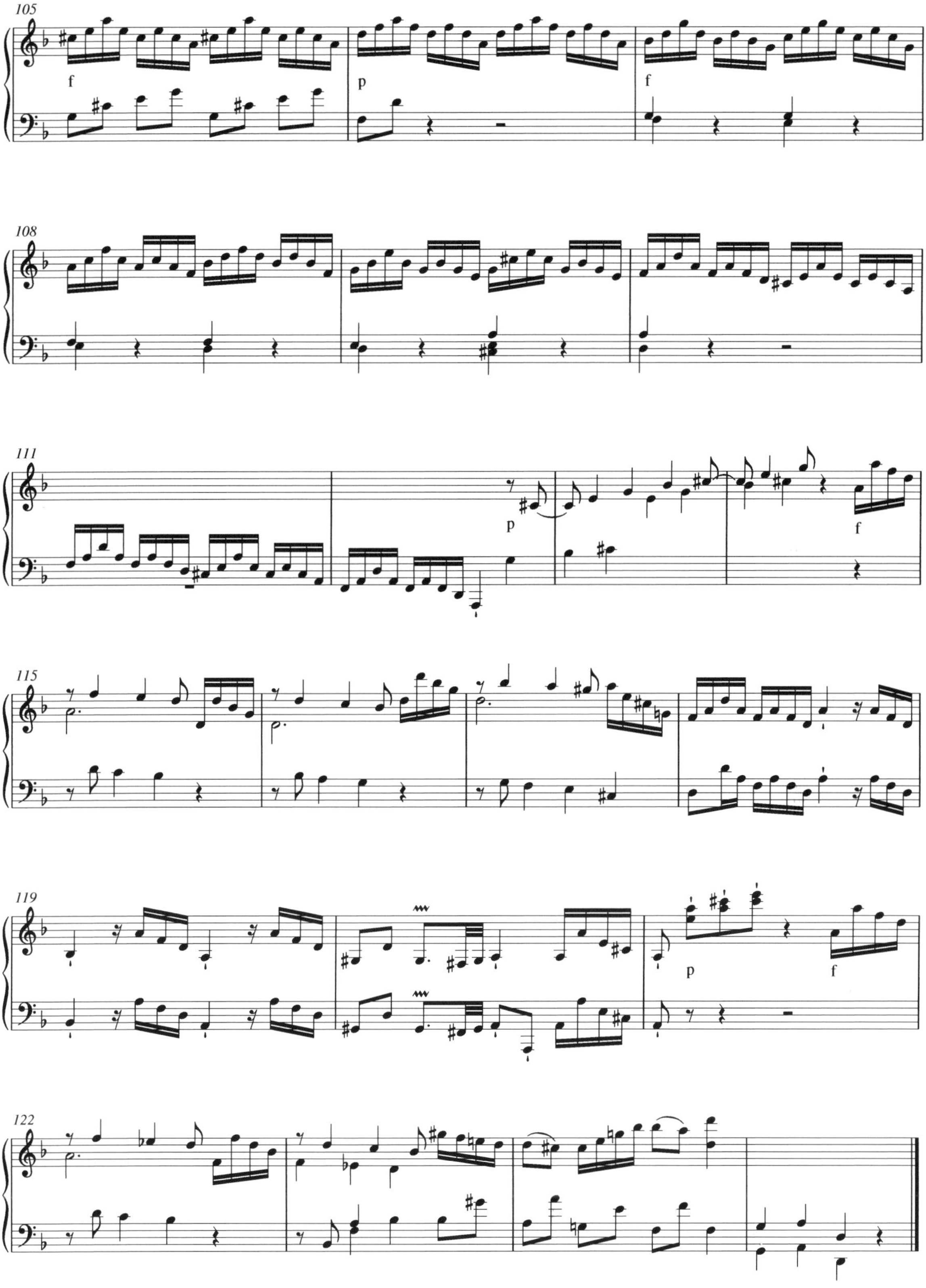
105
f
p
f
108
111
p
f
115
119
p
f
122

Sonata II in E Minor

Fantasia II in C Major

Wq 61/6

Presto di molto

Fantasia in F-sharp Minor

Wq 67

36

CPEB:CW Offprints

1. Six Symphonies for Baron van Swieten, Wq 182
2. *Die Israeliten in der Wüste*, Wq 238
3. Concerto in A Minor, Wq 1
4. Magnificat, Wq 215
5. "Probestücke" Sonatas, Wq 63
6. Concerto in E-flat Major, Wq 165 and Wq 40
7. *Dank-Hymne der Freundschaft*, H 824e
8. *Orchester-Sinfonien mit zwölf obligaten Stimmen*, Wq 183
9. Organ Sonatas and Prelude, Wq 70/2–7
10. *Klopstocks Morgengesang am Schöpfungsfeste*, Wq 239, and Other Chamber Cantatas
11. "Kenner und Liebhaber" Erste Sammlung, Wq 55
12. *Gellerts Geistliche Oden und Lieder mit Melodien*, Wq 194
13. Concerto in A Minor, Wq 170, Wq 26, and Wq 166
14. Passion according to St. Matthew (1769)
15. "Prussian" Sonatas, Wq 48
16. *Gott hat den Herrn auferwecket*, Wq 244
17. Accompanied Sonatas, Wq 89
18. Passion according to St. John (1772)
19. *Cramers übersetzte Psalmen mit Melodien*, Wq 196
20. Concerto in D Major, Wq 13
21. "Kenner und Liebhaber" Collections
22. *Musik am Dankfeste*, H 823
23. "Kenner und Liebhaber" Zweite Sammlung, Wq 56
24. Concerto in G Major, Wq 34 and Wq 169
25. *Oden mit Melodien*, Wq 199
26. Symphony in E Minor, Wq 177–178
27. Concerto in B-flat Major, Wq 164 and Wq 39
28. Quartets for Keyboard, Flute, and Viola, Wq 93–95
29. Concerto in C Minor, Wq 5
30. *Neue Lieder-Melodien*, Wq 200
31. "Kenner und Liebhaber" Dritte Sammlung, Wq 57
32. Concerto in D Minor, Wq 22
33. Sonatina in C Major, Wq 106 and Wq 101
34. Sonatina in D Minor, Wq 107 and Wq 104
35. Sonatina in E-flat Major, Wq 108 and Wq 105
36. Accompanied Sonatas, Wq 90–91
37. Concerto in F Major, Wq 43/1
38. Concerto in D Major, Wq 43/2

39. Concerto in E-flat Major, Wq 43/3

40. Concerto in C Minor, Wq 43/4

41. Concerto in G Major, Wq 43/5

42. Concerto in C Major, Wq 43/6

43. Trios, 1731–1747

44. Trios, 1747–1754

45. Trios, 1755–1787

46. Concerto in E Minor, Wq 24

47. *Auf, schicke dich*, Wq 249

48. "Württemberg" Sonatas, Wq 49

49. Concerto in A Major, Wq 172, Wq 29, and Wq 168

50. *Ich will den Namen des Herrn preisen*, Wq 245

51. Concerto in D Major, Wq 11

52. Concerto in E Major, Wq 14

53. Concerto in B-flat Major, Wq 25

54. Passion according to St. Mark (1774)

55. Passion according to St. Luke (1775)

56. Flute Solos (Wq 123–134)

57. "Leichte" Sonatas, Wq 53

58. "Damen" Sonatas, Wq 54

59. *Sturms geistliche Gesänge mit Melodien*, Wq 197–198

60. Concerto in B-flat Major, Wq 171, Wq 28, and Wq 167

61. "Kenner und Liebhaber" Vierte Sammlung, Wq 58

62. "Kenner und Liebhaber" Fünfte Sammlung, Wq 59
and Rondo in E Minor, Wq 66

63. "Kenner und Liebhaber" Sechste Sammlung, Wq 61
and Fantasia in F-sharp Minor, Wq 67

Made in the USA
Middletown, DE
30 January 2019